Dorothy Y. Revak
November 14, 2000

W9-BZQ-519

Dorothy Y. Revak
November 14, 2000

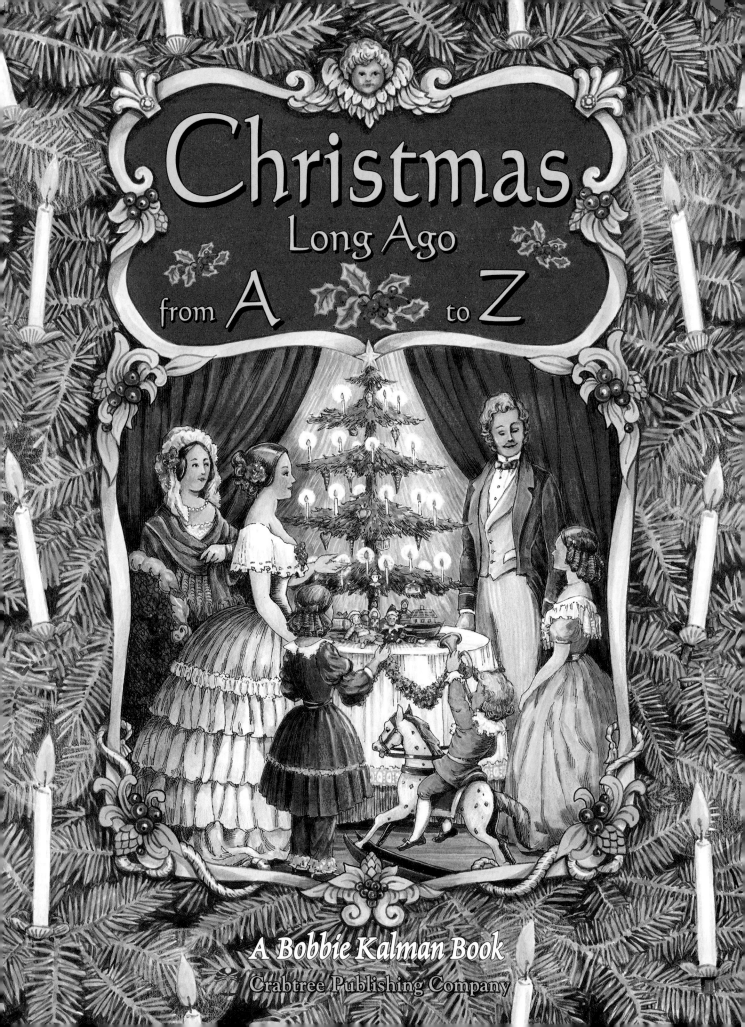

Christmas
Long Ago
from A to Z

A Bobbie Kalman Book

Crabtree Publishing Company

AlphaBasiCs

Created by Bobbie Kalman

To Grandmother, my guardian angel
I know you are always with me!

Author and Editor-in-Chief
Bobbie Kalman

Managing editor
Lynda Hale

Editors
Hannelore Sotzek
John Crossingham

Computer design
Lynda Hale
Robert MacGregor (cover)

Production coordinator
Hannelore Sotzek

Separations and film
Dot 'n Line Image Inc.

Illustrations
Barbara Bedell: cover, title page, all borders, boxes,
    and page decorations, pages 2-3, 5 (top), 6 (top), 7 (top),
    8-13, 17 (bottom), 18-19 (all except Santas in boxes),
    20, 21 (stocking and presents), 23 (bottom), 24 (top
    and bottom left), 26, 27 (top), 30
Antoinette "Cookie" Bortolon: page 17 (top)
Tammy Everts: page 14 (top)
Lisa Smith: page 15 (top)

Photographs and reproductions
Fine Art Photographic Library, London / Art Resource, NY:
    pages 6 (detail), 7 (detail), 21 (detail—bottom left),
    29 (bottom)
Other images by Eyewire, Inc.

Printer
Worzalla Publishing Co.

Crabtree Publishing Company

350 Fifth Avenue	360 York Road, RR 4	73 Lime Walk
Suite 3308	Niagara-on-the-Lake	Headington
New York	Ontario, Canada	Oxford OX3 7AD
N.Y. 10118	L0S 1J0	United Kingdom

Copyright © **1999 CRABTREE PUBLISHING COMPANY**.
All rights reserved. No part of this publication may
be reproduced, stored in a retrieval system or be
transmitted in any form or by any means,
electronic, mechanical,
photocopying, recording,
or otherwise, without
the prior written
permission of Crabtree
Publishing Company.

Cataloging in Publication Data

Kalman, Bobbie
    Christmas long ago from A to Z

(AlphaBasiCs)
Includes index.

ISBN 0-86505-385-5 (library bound)
ISBN 0-86505-415-0 (pbk.)
This book is an alphabetical introduction to Christmas
traditions in the nineteenth century, such as "Christmas
Carols," "Ornaments," and "Toys Under the Tree."

1. Christmas—History—19th century—Juvenile
Literature. [1. Christmas—History—19th century.
2. Alphabet.]
I. Title. II. Series: Kalman, Bobbie. AlphaBasiCs.

GT4985.5.K54 1999   j394.2663   LC 99-22344
                                                            CIP

Contents

is for **angels**. Angels are an important part of Christmas. On the first Christmas, about 2000 years ago, a group of shepherds were watching over their sheep at night. Suddenly, a glorious angel appeared to them. The angel told the shepherds that a very special baby was born that day. His name was Jeshua, and he was God's gift to the world. He is now known as Jesus Christ.

is for **Bethlehem**, the town where Jesus was born. The angel told the shepherds they would find the baby in a stable, lying in a **manger**. Each December 25th, **Christians** celebrate the birth of Jesus Christ. Many people put angels on top of their Christmas tree to remember the Christmas angel, and some have a **creche** (shown left) in their home as a symbol of the stable in Bethlehem.

is for **Christmas carols**. Carols are songs of joy. The French started singing them in the 1300s, but the custom died out. About 150 years ago, people began singing carols again. They sang outside churches and homes. For their songs, carolers received food and a drink called **wassail**. Caroling was called **wassailing**, and the musicians who played Christmas music were called **waits**.

is for **dinner** and **dessert**. Christmas dinner long ago was a feast that included turkey, stuffing, ham, yams, potatoes, and gravy. After dinner, everyone looked forward to the special Christmas dessert—**plum pudding**! Warm brandy was poured over the pudding and lit. When the curtains were drawn, the flaming pudding was brought into the darkened room and served.

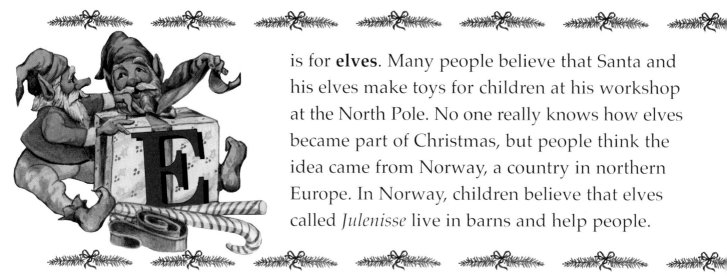

is for **elves**. Many people believe that Santa and his elves make toys for children at his workshop at the North Pole. No one really knows how elves became part of Christmas, but people think the idea came from Norway, a country in northern Europe. In Norway, children believe that elves called *Julenisse* live in barns and help people.

8

At Christmas, Norwegians leave a dessert in the barn for the elves, just as children leave Santa cookies and milk. Perhaps the *Julenisse* travel to the North Pole each year to help Santa. What do you think? Do you know why Santa's workshop is believed to be at the North Pole? The North Pole is mostly ice, so it does not belong to any country. By living at the North Pole, Santa belongs to all the children of the world.

is for **fun** with **family** and **friends**. Christmas week was a time of many activities. Children acted out fairy tales or tried to make each other laugh in a game of Pinch, No Smiling (below). Family members sang and danced and then bundled up for an evening sleigh-ride. On Christmas Eve, children eagerly hung their stockings on the fireplace mantel with the hope that Santa would fill them.

is for **ghost** stories and parlor **games**. Ghost
stories were a popular part of Christmas
long ago. People sat around a flickering fire
telling scary tales. A favorite ghost story was
"A Christmas Carol" by Charles Dickens.
A favorite Christmas game was the Spider
Game. Instead of decorating a tree, some
parents hung "spider webs." The ends of
the streamers led to hidden Christmas gifts.

are for **holly**, **ivy**, and other Christmas decorations that come from nature. Holly is the green plant with red berries that is next to the letter *H*. Ivy is the vine beside *I*. It is a symbol of love. Long ago, people put holly and ivy around their home in winter because they believed the plants had magical powers. They have been used as Christmas decorations ever since.

*Christmas **garlands** were hung around doorways and fireplace mantels. Garlands were made by tying together branches and adding apples, cones, nuts, holly, and bows. Garlands were first hung by the **Druids**, who lived almost 2000 years ago. They believed garlands brought good luck.*

The Christmas rose, shown above, blooms in December. There is a story about a young girl in Bethlehem who was sad because she had no gift to take to the baby Jesus. An angel appeared to her and scattered roses on her path to the manger. She brought them to Jesus as her gift. Christmas roses, as well as apples and nuts, shown below, were used as decorations on the first Christmas trees.

When settlers first arrived in North America they found that no holly grew there, but the cranberry plant had similar red berries. The settlers used this plant to decorate their homes and dress their Christmas turkey.

Kissing balls were bunches of mistletoe and holly that were tied together into a ball and hung in doorways. When a young woman stood under the doorway, a young man could "steal" a kiss from her.

Mistletoe was thought to be a plant of peace. In England, people shook hands or kissed under the mistletoe at Christmastime. The kissing custom is still popular today.

Pomanders were popular Christmas decorations in the 1800s. They looked good and made a house smell wonderful! Children could easily make one by sticking cloves into an orange and tying a satin ribbon around it.

The poinsettia is a popular Christmas plant because of its red and green color. It was brought to the United States from Mexico by Joel Poinsett in the 1800s. In a Mexican Christmas legend, a boy named Pablo wanted to offer a gift to Mary, the mother of Jesus. He could find only weeds to give. When he laid them at her statue, the weeds turned into the beautiful poinsettia plant.

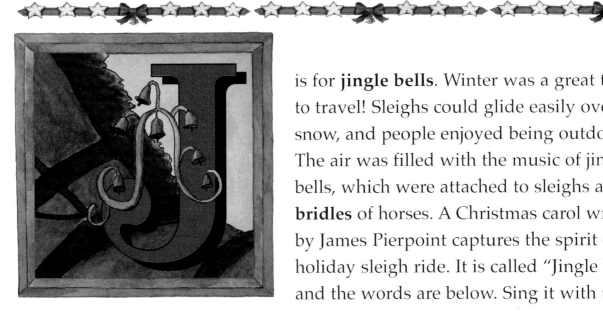

is for **jingle bells**. Winter was a great time to travel! Sleighs could glide easily over the snow, and people enjoyed being outdoors. The air was filled with the music of jingling bells, which were attached to sleighs and the **bridles** of horses. A Christmas carol written by James Pierpoint captures the spirit of a holiday sleigh ride. It is called "Jingle Bells," and the words are below. Sing it with us!

Dashing through the snow
In a one-horse open sleigh,
O'er the fields we go
Laughing all the way;
Bells on bobtail ring,
Making spirits bright;
Oh, what fun it is to sing
A sleighing song tonight!

Jingle bells! Jingle bells!
Jingle all the way!
Oh, what fun it is to ride
In a one-horse open sleigh!
Jingle bells! Jingle bells!
Jingle all the way!
Oh, what fun it is to ride
In a one-horse open sleigh!

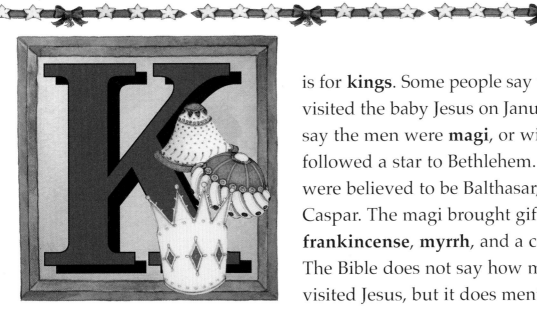

is for **kings**. Some people say that three kings visited the baby Jesus on January 6th. Others say the men were **magi**, or wise men, who followed a star to Bethlehem. Their names were believed to be Balthasar, Melchior, and Caspar. The magi brought gifts to Jesus—**frankincense**, **myrrh**, and a casket of gold. The Bible does not say how many magi visited Jesus, but it does mention three gifts.

is for **lights**. Christmas is often called a "festival of lights" because people decorate trees, homes, and churches with lights and candles. The custom of placing candles in windows started in Ireland. The candles were lit on Christmas Eve and burned until January 6th. People believed that the lighted candles helped Mary and Joseph, the parents of Jesus, find Bethlehem.

is for **Martin Luther**, a man who lived in Germany in the 1500s. People believe that he started the custom of putting lights on trees. On an evening walk, Martin Luther noticed the stars shining through the branches of the snow-covered trees, making the trees look as if they were lighted by hundreds of candles! He wanted to share the joy he felt with his children. What do you think he did next?

is for "...**night** before Christmas," part of the first line of a poem written by Clement Moore in 1822. In his poem, called "A Visit from St. Nicholas," Moore described Santa Claus in a new way. Read the poem and then turn to pages 24 and 25 to find out how Moore's Santa was different from the St. Nicholas of long ago and the Santa Claus of today.

A Visit from St. Nicholas
by Clement Clarke Moore

'Twas the night before Christmas,
    when all through the house
Not a creature was stirring, not even a mouse.
The stockings were hung by the chimney with care,
In the hopes that St. Nicholas soon would be there.
    The children were nestled all snug in their beds,
    While visions of sugarplums danced in their heads;
    And Mamma in her kerchief, and I in my cap,
Had just settled our brains for a long winter's nap—
    When out on the lawn there arose such a clatter
    I sprang from my bed to see what was the matter.

Away to the window I flew like a flash,
Tore open the shutters and threw up the sash.
The moon on the breast of the new-fallen snow
Gave a luster of midday to the objects below;
When what to my wondering eyes should appear
But a miniature sleigh and eight tiny reindeer,
With a little old driver, so lively and quick,
I knew in a moment it must be St. Nick!
More rapid than eagles his coursers they came,
And he whistled and shouted and called them by name.
"Now Dasher! now, Dancer! now Prancer and Vixen!
On, Comet! on Cupid! on Donder and Blitzen!

To the top of the porch, to the top of the wall,
Now, dash away, dash away, dash away, all!"
As dry leaves that before the wild hurricane fly,
When they meet with an obstacle mount to the sky,
So up to the housetop the coursers they flew,
With a sleigh full of toys—and St. Nicholas, too.
And then in a twinkling, I heard on the roof
The prancing and pawing of each little hoof.
As I drew in my head and was turning around,
Down the chimney St. Nicholas came with a bound.

He was dressed all in fur from his head to his foot,
And his clothes were all tarnished with ashes and soot.
A bundle of toys he had flung on his back,
And he looked like a peddler just opening his pack.
His eyes, how they twinkled! His dimples, how merry!
His cheeks were like roses, his nose like a cherry;
His droll little mouth was drawn up like a bow,
And the beard on his chin was as white as the snow.
The stump of his pipe he held tight in his teeth,
And the smoke, it encircled his head like a wreath.

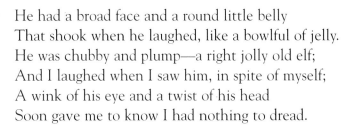

He had a broad face and a round little belly
That shook when he laughed, like a bowlful of jelly.
He was chubby and plump—a right jolly old elf;
And I laughed when I saw him, in spite of myself;
A wink of his eye and a twist of his head
Soon gave me to know I had nothing to dread.

He spoke not a word, but went straight to work,
And filled all the stockings; then turned with a jerk,
And laying his finger aside of his nose,
And giving a nod, up the chimney he rose.
He sprang to his sleigh, to his team gave a whistle,
And away they all flew like the down of a thistle.
But I heard him exclaim, ere he drove out of sight,
"Happy Christmas to all, and to all a good night!"

O is for **ornaments**, or tree decorations. The first Christmas tree decorations were candles, apples, roses, pine cones, and nuts. Some people hung cookies and candy on their tree, but these edible ornaments quickly disappeared. Other families decorated their tree with **miniatures** of furniture and other objects. A star or angel was the tree's crowning glory!

*Some of the first store-bought ornaments were colorful glass balls called **kugels**. They were made in Germany.*

*Ornaments called **cornucopias** were shaped like cones and held nuts, candies, and fruit. Cornucopia means "horn of plenty." There were plenty of goodies in this cornucopia!*

Dresdens, such as this lion, looked like metal ornaments, but they were actually made of cardboard. The cardboard was covered with silver, gold, or copper paint.

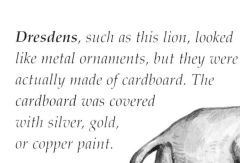

is for **presents**. Giving presents at Christmas-time started with the shepherds who brought gifts of fruit and honey to Jesus. The Magi also brought presents to show their respect. For years, children received small unwrapped gifts such as fruit or mittens for Christmas. In the late 1800s, people started wrapping presents, and many children received toys for Christmas, just as they do today.

is for **quiz**. Take this quiz to calculate your Christmas IQ. The answers are in this book.

1. What were Christmas musicians called? 2. Where was Jesus born? 3. What was a favorite Christmas dessert? 4. Who wrote Jingle Bells? 5. Name Santa's reindeer. 6. What does the X in Xmas stand for? 7. Who gave the first Christmas gifts? 8. What was a popular Christmas Eve story? 9. Where is Santa's workshop? 10. Who put lights on the first Christmas tree? **If you score: 8-10, you are an angel; 5-7, you are an elf; 1-4, you are a kugel!**

is for **reindeer**. Reindeer live in the Arctic, near the North Pole. In his poem, "A Visit from St. Nicholas," Clement Moore wrote that Santa's sleigh was pulled by eight reindeer: Dasher, Dancer, Prancer, Vixen, Comet, Cupid, Donder, and Blitzen. Rudolph, the red-nosed reindeer, did not join Santa's team until 25 years later!

The idea that Santa's sleigh was pulled by reindeer probably started in Norway and Sweden, where these animals live.

is for **Santa Claus**, whose name comes from **St. Nicholas**, a bishop who lived in Turkey about 1000 years ago. In an old legend, St. Nicholas saved three girls from becoming slaves by putting gold coins in their shoes. Children in Europe believed he brought their Christmas gifts.

St. Nicholas was pictured wearing a bishop's robe and riding a horse. He was known as Sinter Klaas, Kriss Kringle, and Pelznickel. Father Christmas, shown below, was the British Santa. The early Santas looked like the three shown here, but today's Santa looks much more jolly, like the one on the next page.

How are all these Santas different from the one described in the poem on page 19?

T is for **tree** and **toys**, and U is for **under** the tree. Queen Victoria's husband, Prince Albert, brought the custom of decorating Christmas trees from Germany to England. The custom then spread to North America. The Royal Family also made it popular to give children toys for Christmas.

is for **visiting**. Visiting relatives and friends was a big part of the Christmas season. Families traveled far to see one another. Friends organized **visiting parties**, at which a group of people surprised a family with food, gifts, and music. Children also liked visiting friends. They went to parties, where they danced and played games. What a merry time was Christmas long ago!

is for **wishes**. How do you communicate your Christmas wishes? Do you write a letter to Santa Claus, or do you tell him your wishes in person the way the little boy in the picture is doing? Do you remember to wish good things for others as well? By wishing good things for others and doing good deeds each day, you can keep the spirit of Christmas alive in your heart all year long!

is for **Xmas**. Many people write Christmas as Xmas because they want to remember the true meaning of the holiday. In the Greek alphabet, *X* stands for Christ. Some Christians write Xmas because *X* also stands for the cross—the symbol of the Christian religion. No matter how Christmas is spelled, many people go to church on Xmas Eve or Xmas Day to celebrate the birth of Jesus Christ.

is for New **Year**. People long ago celebrated New Year's Eve with family and friends, just as they do today. They danced the old year away and sang in the New Year. At midnight, the church bells rang, and people gathered in a circle to sing "Auld Lang Syne." On New Year's Day, young men competed to see who could visit the most women. They left **calling cards** as proof of their visit.

Words to know

Bethlehem The town in Israel where Jesus was born

bishop An important person who works for the Christian church

bridle A leather harness put on a horse

calling card A small card with a person's name written on it

Christians People who follow the religious teachings of Jesus Christ

cornucopia A horn of plenty filled with fruits, nuts, and candies

creche A model of the stable, animals, and people present at the birth of Jesus Christ

Druids Priests who lived in Britain and France 2000 years ago

frankincense A perfume made from tropical trees

Luther, Martin A German religious leader who founded the Lutheran Church

manger An open wooden box that holds food for animals

miniature A small copy of a large object

myrrh A substance found in trees that is used in perfume

Prince Albert The German husband of Queen Victoria who helped make Christmas into a special time for children

St. Nicholas A Turkish bishop who lived 1000 years ago and was said to bring gifts to children; another name for Santa Claus

Index

1 2 3 4 5 6 7 8 9 0 Printed in the U.S.A. 8 7 6 5 4 3 2 1 0 9